The BERRY Book

MOLLY'S JAM

BY GAIL GIBBONS

Holiday House / New York

To Joan Whiting

Special thanks to
Dr. David Yarborough,
Blueberry Specialist and Associate Professor
of Horticulture at the University of Maine, Orono, Maine.

Library of Congress Cataloging-in-Publication Data
Gibbons, Gail.
The berry book / Gail Gibbons.
p. cm.
Summary: Describes different types of berries and how they grow.
Includes recipes with berry ingredients.
ISBN 0-8234-1697-6 (hardcover)
1. Berries—Juvenile literature. 2. Cookery (Berries)—Juvenile literature.
[1. Berries. 2. Cookery (Berries)] I. Title.

SB381 .G53 2002
634'.7—dc21
2001040602

CRANBERRIES

WILD STRAWBERRIES

BOYSENBERRIES

WINTERGREEN BERRIES

STRAWBERRIES

GOOSEBERRIES

RASPBERRIES

BLUEBERRIES

BLACKBERRIES

Berries are a type of fruit. They grow on different kinds of plants. Berries grow to be many different shapes and sizes.

BUNCHBERRIES

ELDERBERRIES

MISTLETOE BERRIES

CURRANTS

Some berries are POISONOUS. BE CERTAIN to show all berries to an adult before eating them.

HOLLY BERRIES

SNOWBERRIES

Some berries are soft. Others are hard. Many berries are edible, and others are not.

WINTERGREEN BERRIES

BLUEBERRIES

HOLLY BERRIES

STRAWBERRIES

Different kinds of berries grow in different climates. Berries grow on every continent except Antarctica.

RASPBERRIES

POKEBERRIES

BLUEBERRIES

CRANBERRIES

Berries have been in existence for millions of years. They continue to be eaten by birds, wild animals, and people.

About 400 years ago, the first American colonists were taught by Native Americans about the wild berries growing in their region. The colonists learned how to identify and use them.

WILD RASPBERRIES

WILD BLACKBERRIES

Today, many people still enjoy picking and eating wild berries.

Wild berries
are smaller than
cultivated berries.

WILD STRAWBERRY
PLANTS

CULTIVATED
STRAWBERRY
PLANTS

Some berries are grown in gardens. They are called cultivated
berries.

CULTIVATED
STRAWBERRY FIELD

CULTIVATED BLUEBERRY FIELD

Cultivated berries also are grown in nurseries and on farms.

BLUEBERRY RAKE

BLUEBERRY
HARVESTING

CRANBERRY
HARVESTING

Cultivated berries are harvested in different ways. Sometimes they are handpicked or raked. Sometimes machines are used to harvest them.

Berries may be sold at roadside stands.

Most berries are shipped to stores. There are fresh berries and frozen berries. There are many berry products.

We eat STRAWBERRIES.

BLOSSOM

In the early spring tiny flowers, called strawberry blossoms, begin to bloom on strawberry plants.

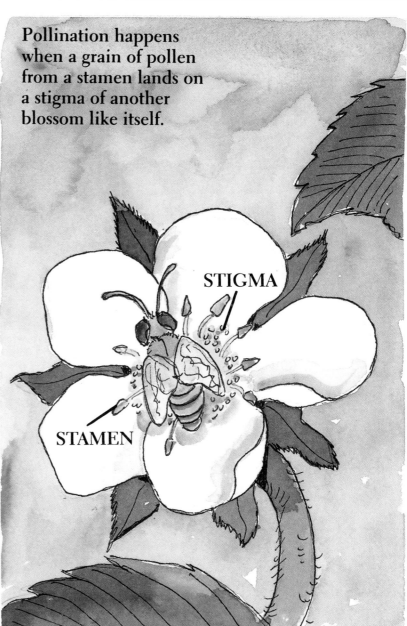

Pollination happens when a grain of pollen from a stamen lands on a stigma of another blossom like itself.

STIGMA

STAMEN

Each blossom must be pollinated in order for a strawberry to grow. Strawberry blossoms are usually pollinated by insects or by the wind.

After a while, the petals begin to die. Small green strawberries begin to grow.

They grow bigger and bigger. Finally they ripen to become red, juicy strawberries. They are so good to eat!

Other common berries we eat are RASPBERRIES and BLACKBERRIES...

CULTIVATED BLACKBERRIES

CULTIVATED RASPBERRIES

WILD RASPBERRIES

WILD BLACKBERRIES

DRUPELETS (DROOP•lets)

Raspberries and blackberries grow on thorny bushes. A raspberry and a blackberry are made up of cells called drupelets.

BLUEBERRIES...

WILD BLUEBERRIES

CULTIVATED BLUEBERRIES

CULTIVATED BLUEBERRY BUSH

Blueberries grow on blueberry bushes. Blueberries are round and smooth.

and CRANBERRIES, too.

WILD CRANBERRIES

CULTIVATED CRANBERRIES

A BOG is a wet area.

Cranberry sauce is served with turkey.

Cranberries grow in bogs. Cranberries are firm and red.

We eat GOOSEBERRIES...

Gooseberries grow on bushes in dry places. Some gooseberries have stripes. Careful…their stems are thorny.

CURRANTS...

Currants grow on bushes in warm, moist places. They are small and shiny. Once they have been dried, they look like small raisins and are good to eat.

and WINTERGREEN BERRIES, too.

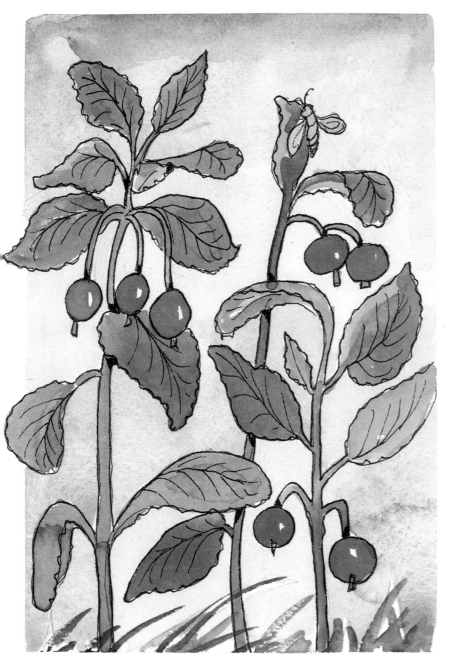

Wintergreen leaves can be used to make tea.

Wintergreen berries grow on small plants with evergreen leaves and ripen in the fall. The oil from wintergreen berries is used to flavor candy.

Some common berries we don't eat are BAYBERRIES...

Bayberry bushes have been known to grow as high as 40 feet (12 m).
Often the oil from bayberries is used to scent candles.

MISTLETOE and HOLLY, too.

MISTLETOE BERRIES

HOLLY BERRIES

An old custom is that if someone wants to be kissed, they stand under mistletoe.

MISTLETOE

HOLLY

Mistletoe is used at Christmas as a symbol of joy. Red holly berries and their green leaves are the colors of Christmas. They are often used as decorations.

Some towns have strawberry festivals.

Many people go to country fairs. Sometimes awards are given for the best tasting strawberry jam, blueberry pie, and other foods.

How to grow your own STRAWBERRIES.

1. In the early spring, choose a bright, sunny place with fertile soil and dig a garden plot.

2. Buy young strawberry plants at a garden nursery or store.

3. Dig holes about 18 inches (45cm) apart and just deep enough to cover the roots. Place one plant in each hole and add soil to keep it in place.

4. Water the plants about three times a week. Strawberry plants need lots of water to grow juicy berries.

5. It takes about two months for strawberry blossoms to grow into red, ripe berries. Then they can be harvested.

6. In northern climates, strawberry plants should be covered to protect them through the cold winter months while they are dormant.

DORMANT means alive but not growing.

7. When it gets warm in the spring, the strawberry plants will grow and make new strawberries.

Strawberry plants often grow **RUNNERS** to make new plants.

How to make a BLUEBERRY PIE...

1. Rinse and clean 3 cups (710 ml) of blueberries.

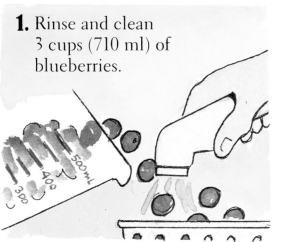

2. Add 2 tablespoons (30 ml) of flour, 3/4 cup (178 ml) of sugar, and 1/8 teaspoon (.60 ml) of salt to the berries.

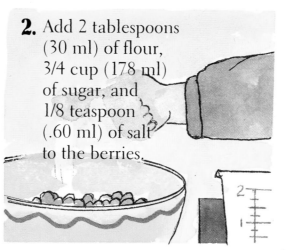

3. Mix well.

4. Spread pastry dough into a 9 inch (22.5cm) pie tin.

5. Add the berry mixture and sprinkle with lemon juice.

6. Add dots of butter on top.

7. Put on the top layer of pastry dough and poke some holes in the top.

8. Bake for about 45 minutes at 425°F (218°C).

STRAWBERRY JAM and RASPBERRY ICE CREAM.

STRAWBERRY JAM

1. Put 1 quart (946 ml) of rinsed strawberries in a pan.

2. Add 1 cup (236 ml) of sugar and stir.

3. Heat over a low flame until the mixture begins to boil. Boil for 3 minutes.

4. Add another cup (236 ml) of sugar and stir.

5. Cook and stir the mixture again for about 3 minutes.

6. Cool the jam until it is ready to eat. Store it in a jar in a cool, dry place.

RASPBERRY ICE CREAM

1. Mix together 2 cups (473 ml) of light cream, 2 cups (473 ml) of raspberries, 1/4 teaspoon (1.23 ml) of salt and 1/4 cup (60 ml) of sugar.

2. Put the mixture into a bowl, cover it and place in a freezer until it is firm.

BLACKBERRIES

HUCKLEBERRIES

WILD STRAWBERRIES

MAHONIA BERRIES

BLUEBERRIES

SALMON BERRIES

BUFFALO BERRIES

GOOSEBERRIES

Berries are beautiful. They are fun to pick. Berries are nutritious and delicious, too.

BERRIES...BERRIES...BERRIES...

The Pilgrims thought the white flowers of cranberries looked like the heads of birds called cranes. They called the plant crane-berry, which became cranberry.

Scientists classify grapes, bananas, cucumbers, tomatoes and many other fruits as berries, too.

More than 500 million pounds (227 million kg) of cranberries are harvested each year in North America.

Early Americans chewed wintergreen leaves as a breath freshener.

In the Arctic, tiny strawberry plants grow close to the ground, and ripen in the sunshine of the Arctic summer.

The state of Maine has a blueberry festival each year in the town of Union. There is a blueberry pancake breakfast and a blueberry pie eating contest.

Throughout history berries have not only been used as food. They've been used as medicine, as dyes, and to make ink.

Huckleberries look like small blueberries. They are used to make pies and jams.

The United States and Canada lead all other countries in the growing of strawberries and blueberries.

Cranberries were one of the many native foods served at the first Thanksgiving at Plymouth, Massachusetts, in October, 1621.

About 80% of all strawberries grown in the United States come from California.